Written by Robin Loisch
Illustrated by Deb Johnson

3058002100000270

God told Adam and Eve they could eat from every tree in the garden except one.
I tricked Eve into eating from the wrong tree. What am I?

Color the pieces that have dots to find out. (Genesis 3:1–13)

God told Noah to build an ark to save his family and the animals from the flood. When the rain stopped, Noah sent me to find dry land. What am I?

Color the pieces that have dots to find out. (Genesis 8:6–12)

Jacob was cooking when Esau came home. Esau was so hungry!
Esau sold his rights as the firstborn son to Jacob for me. What am I?

Color the pieces that have dots to find out. (Genesis 25:29–34)

Jacob loved his son Joseph the most. He gave me to Joseph as a gift.
Joseph's brothers were jealous when they saw me. What am I?

Color the pieces that have dots to find out. (Genesis 37:1–4)

A bad Pharaoh said all Hebrew baby boys had to be thrown in the river.
One mother used me to hide her son. What am I?

Color the pieces that have dots to find out. (Exodus 2:1–8)

God's army marched around the city walls. I was played loudly, and the army shouted. Then the walls of Jericho fell down! What am I?

Color the pieces that have dots to find out. (Joshua 6:1–20)

When King Saul wasn't feeling well, David played me.
Then the king felt much better. What am I?

Color the pieces that have dots to find out. (1 Samuel 16:14–23)

A poor widow didn't have much oil or flour, but she made me for Elijah. Then God made it so her oil and flour did not run out until the famine was over. What am I?

Color the pieces that have dots to find out. (1 Kings 17:7–16)

The king chose Esther to be the new queen.
Then he placed me on her head. What am I?

Color the pieces that have dots to find out. (Esther 2:15–18)

When Baby Jesus was born, Mary used me as a bed for Him.
What am I?

Color the pieces that have dots to find out. (Luke 2:4–7)

Some wise men in the east saw me in the sky.
They followed me all the way to where Jesus lived. What am I?

Color the pieces that have dots to find out. (Matthew 2:1–12)

John the Baptist lived in the wilderness. He told everyone Jesus was coming soon. For food, he ate me along with wild honey. What am I?

Color the pieces that have dots to find out. (Matthew 3:1–6)

Jesus had been preaching from a boat. When He was done, Jesus told Simon to put his fishing nets in the water. Simon caught me and many more like me! What am I?

Color the pieces that have dots to find out. (Luke 5:1–11)

Jesus rode me into Jerusalem. People were so excited!
They waved palm branches and shouted, "Hosanna!" What am I?

Color the pieces that have dots to find out. (Matthew 21:1–11)

Jesus carried me to a sad place. Then soldiers nailed Jesus to me. Jesus died for our sins, but three days later He was alive again! Because Jesus did this, we can go to heaven someday! What am I?

Color the pieces that have dots to find out. (John 19:16–18)